"Leading change is an every-day reality; in every business and in every sector. Within tightly regulated industries, leaders must take care to introduce change whilst maintaining and improving standards. In this book, John and Steve have pooled their knowledge and experience working within the nuclear industry to offer a roadmap for leaders creating, delivering and sustaining change. They show that by deploying some simple techniques, understanding the human condition in all its complexity and acknowledging our 'beautiful constraints', we can, nevertheless, take our people through a transformational and sustainable change journey."

Peter Prozesky
CEO, World Association of Nuclear Operators

ABOUT THE AUTHORS

John Herbert and Steve Marriott are leadership consultants, obsessive about developing leaders and confident that neuroscience research is a significant factor in reshaping how we define leadership, inspire leaders and design effective leadership development programs.

They understand that the recent breakthroughs in cognitive science can lead and influence mindful change and that sustainable organizational transformation has got to take into account the physiological nature of the brain.

Mr Badger's experiences are based upon their consultancy work over a period of 15 years and Mr Badger Moves Home is really an amalgamation of the many leadership development interventions they've created and the golden threads that have emerged as they honed their skills delivering to senior leaders across the UK and Europe.

Coming together with a group of like-minded colleagues as CTL Consult they continue to deliver award winning leadership development specialising in leaders operating within regulated environments.

Our Inspiration

In 2008, early groundwork began on the proposed site of Hinkley Point C, the UK's first new-build nuclear power station for over two decades.

Preliminary surveys discovered a large community – a 'cete' – of badgers living within the proposed perimeter of the power station, which would have to be moved before work on the build could commence.

Badger colonies are protected by UK law and special permission must be granted to relocate them. With permission granted, EDF Energy engaged a team of environmental experts to construct a new den, some 1.5km away from the build site. This new den was to be degradable to encourage the relocated badgers to retain their natural habits and instincts.

Upon completion of the build, the team were then set the task of permanently relocating the entire badger colony from their historic home to the new 'Badger-opolis' with the move creating as little upheaval and disturbance to the colony as possible.

Mr Badger Moves Home was inspired by the simple and careful steps taken by the environmental team in the process of 'making it easier' for the badgers to move home rather than forcing the move through more antiquated methods.

In discussions with groups of leaders from various industries and sectors, we've been amazed at the reception our tale receives. Not only does the tale captivate even the most discerning leaders, our discussions of the very simple actions the environmental team took have uncovered a number of remarkable similarities with our workplaces and workgroups.

The Somerset Levels are an ancient fertile place where animals and mankind have lived side by side for thousands of years. The cold winds that blow down from the Mendips and Exmoor hills, or sweep in from the murky Bristol Channel, rustle the vast swathes of reed beds and sweep across pastures. This scene is broken occasionally by small mounds in the marshy ground that both mankind and badgers have made to secure themselves warm and dry places to live and to avoid the annual floods caused by water cascading down from the surrounding moorland.

Under a conspicuously new mound in the centre of the levels, we find Badger and Owl sitting in armchairs, their feet extended towards the hearth, drinking cider from earthenware mugs and eating warm butter-soaked crumpets; as the wind whistles and the rain pours down outside.

"How are you finding the new place then, Badger?" asks Owl looking carefully at him over her reading glasses.

"You know, it's not half bad. This fire draws extremely well, the store cupboard is full, and the new walls are dry and smooth; one hell of an improvement on the wattle and daub that we had in the old place."

"What about the rest of the family?"

"Well, there's been a few moans about the move and a few have gone back to look at the old place but, got to say that most of those have died down, what with the free food and the extra space for us to make the place our own."

Getting into his stride Badger leaned forward and threw another log on the fire.

"Let me tell you how it all happened, Owl. You'll never believe it!"

Owl leaned back in her chair. She'd heard these stories from Badger before so knew that an extra mouthful of crumpet was called for.

"It all happened about six months ago," said Badger. "As you know, there had been quite a lot of movement from them Umans over the past few months; blooming great big machines passing close to the old den in the day, lights on at night, and constant changes to our old footpaths.

Most of the older folk in the family said we should all keep our heads down as stuff like this had happened before a couple of times; apparently once sixty years ago and then again around twenty years after that.

Folklore has it that both times the family had simply kept themselves to themselves, trained a beady eye on them Umans, and made sure that everyone stuck together."

"So what did you do?" said Owl.

"Well you know me, I like to have a look at what's going on out there and one evening I swung on my haversack as usual and decided to head off on my own towards the woods behind Shurton; it's always been a lush spot up there for worms. It was a still night for once and when I'd dodged around the machinery them Umans had left around the patch I headed off on the path. Blow me if pretty soon I didn't smell something tasty in front of me!"

"What was it?" asked Owl sitting forward. "A single delicious honey-covered ball of sweet chestnuts!" said Badger.

"And what did you do?"

"Blooming ate it, of course," said Badger and smiled. "Not exactly enough for a meal, mind you, but very welcome on a cold night, I can tell you."

"Did you carry on to Shurton?" said Owl, not quite knowing where this story was going.

"Well, Owl, I was going to," said Badger, "but I caught a whiff of honey on the air and blow me if ten yards down the old path towards Cross Elms Hill, I didn't find another one of those little beauties smack bang in the middle of the track. Do you know that I found myself tracking these sweet chestnuts all night and by midnight I found myself in Cross Elms Woods, which is where I made my big discovery."

"What was that?" asked Owl, carefully removing a slug from the lip of her cider mug that Badger had thoughtfully placed on the edge as a garnish.

"This place," said Badger extending his clawed arms and waving them gleefully around and pointing at the room.

"Did you go straight in?" asked Owl her interest aroused by this point.

"Well, I bravely put my nose around the door, sniffed the smell of new wood glue, and scarpered home!"

"It's about a mile-and-a-half back from there and when I got home I found most of the family sorting the old bedding from the day before outside of our old gaff. Well, Owl, you can imagine their responses when I told them what sort of night I'd had. Some said that it was a one-off, others told me to stick to our usual paths and that no good would come from heading off to Cross Elms, and most just ignored me and got on with their chores for the night.

Still, the next night I thought I'd set off for Shurton again and blow me if there wasn't another honey-covered sweet chestnut exactly where it had been the night before. I thought to myself that my brother, Arthur, wouldn't mind a few sweet chestnuts so I went back into the den and caught him just as he was going off for a walk himself.

'Why not come with me?' I said. 'If it's anything like last night then there's more than enough for two of us.'

He took a bit of persuading but in the end, he lumbered on with me and once again we found ourselves nicely full of chestnuts and peering into the new den in Cross Elms Hill Wood. This time I went in and that's when I made the big discovery."

"What was that?" said Owl the warm cider by this time making her eyes widen and her legs distinctly wobbly.

"A gert pile of sweet chestnuts in a store cupboard deep into this lovely and nearly finished den. What was strange, mind you, was that I couldn't smell badgers in any of the rooms. It looked like no one had ever been in there before. I couldn't smell the Mangles from Stringston or the Whollops from Kilton way so it was clear Arthur and I were the first ones in. 'Lush!' we thought.

When we got back to the den that night, Arthur and I got the whole family together and told them what had happened. A few nights later, when I came to pull my boots on and head out, a few of the family had decided to go with me. Do you know by the end of the month we were all making the trek to Cross Elms; a long line of us stretched out in the dark hunting for chestnuts and fairly skipping at the prospect of the store of nuts that we knew was waiting for us when we arrived here.

Do you know that by the end of the month I was a bit fed up with having to walk the mile

or so back to the old place and one night I had a look in some of the rooms on the way to the new store and noticed that some excellent beds had been provided in some of the rooms. It didn't take much effort to drop my bag off my shoulder and give that bed a try. What a beautiful night's sleep; no traffic, no Umans, and plenty of food. I was living the dream.

Of course, when Arthur found out I was staying over at Cross Elms he decided to do the same and within a few weeks around five of us had decided to stay at Cross Elms, bringing our belongings and a few pictures for the walls to make the place a home from home.

Got to say that when I did pop home for some jumpers, my best pipe, and my slippers, the old place looked a bit threadbare. I hadn't noticed how hard it had been to keep warm. The noise from them Umans had kept me awake all day and the thought of my nice new wood burner and the food store meant that I was in pretty quick, collected my stuff, and was back to Cross Elms before the sun rose. Then a strange thing happened," said Badger.

"What was that?" said Owl who'd begun to look thoughtful.

"The nuts on the path down to the old den dried up."

"Really?" said Owl.

"Yes, a couple of the family who used to scout back to the old home reported this one night. Of course, not many of us took much notice but interestingly enough even stranger things started to happen. Well, old Jethro, who had been the longest at the old place, thought he would saunter back down the hill and have a look at the old den. He was never convinced that we'd made the right decision and to listen to him you would have thought that we'd lived in a palace rather than the hole that it most certainly was.

When he got down to the edge of our old patch

he found a blooming great fence was blocking
his way on the old track."

"What did he do?" asked Owl.

"Well, he tried digging down to go under, the
way we've all been taught, but found that the
fence went underground much further than any
fence we've ever seen before. Pretty soon he was
running out of puff and so, shaking his fist at
the fence, he made his way back to Cross Elms.

Worse than that, the Umans had put a door in
the fence that a few of the family had used and
one night they found it had stuck tight and they

couldn't get back to the old place.

When he got back to Cross Elms he got a few
of the older badgers together and, by God, did
they kick up a stink. They wanted us to go
back down to the fence and dig our way back
through to the old place. Got to say, my heart
wasn't in it and what with the winter drawing
in, the changes we'd made to the place, and
time for our sleep season to start, not many of
us were keen to go. Even Jethro himself looked
a bit half-hearted after he'd sat down in front of
the fire and eaten a few nuts.

'Let's wait till the spring,' he said. 'That's a time
when badgers take action.'

"Do you know, Owl, that by this spring, most
of us had forgotten the old place. When the
news came from the crows that – looking from
the edge of the wood – it appeared that the
Umans had put a hut smack bang where the
den had been, not many of us were worried.

So, Owl, what do you make of that then?" said
Badger leaning back in his chair with his arms
folded behind his head.

Owl stood up by the fireplace and looked
thoughtfully into the flames.

"Clever folk these Umans, aren't they?" said Owl.

"What do you mean?" said Badger sitting up for the first time.

"Well, let me explain…" said Owl.

Owl went to the fire and grabbed a small piece of charcoal and started to write on Badgers' new walls! At the same time, Badger fished out an old notebook and chewed on the end of a pencil to make it sharp. He knew that once Owl got going there would be some interesting thoughts that he would want to remember so he'd better write them down.

"OK, Badger, tell me, what are badgers like?"

"Well," said Badger. "One thing I know about us badgers is that we like to live in families. Having your kind around you is comforting. You know what I mean?"

"Certainly," said Owl, turning to write.

They live in family groups

"As you know, Badger, most of your kind live in dens of up to twenty-five and these are typically a series of extended families. Many of the Umans also establish teams of around this number and they also find that once they're established and stable then strong bonds will develop between individuals. Some of the recent studies have shown that Uman brains, like badgers, have evolved to live in groups of this size."

"Badgers like to follow routines," said Owl.

Badger nodded.

They're comfortable with routine; they're 'sett' in their ways!

"They use the same paths at the same time and will literally bulldoze new obstacles out of the way if they come across them. Umans are remarkably the same with a brain that's been designed to work on autopilot whenever possible, keeping their ability to think through complex issues on tap for when it might be required."

They can be fierce when cornered

"You badgers have a fearsome reputation for being aggressive when you're cornered. An intruder in the den or a possible predator that comes across you whilst you're out foraging will be met with a sharp set of claws and teeth as well as immense strength for your size. Umans are no different if they find themselves threatened. For example, maintaining the status quo is something that they will fight for, admittedly not often with teeth and claws but with any other tool at their disposal."

They see the world in black and white

"Believe it or not, Badger, for Umans, the world is not how you see it."

Badger snorted.

"Because you badgers have a liking for going out at night, your eyes are developed to see well in reduced light; as a result, you perceive the world in black and white. For Umans, the world is multi-coloured during the day and pretty dark at night. Obviously, this is a bit of a play on words as well, as both Badgers and Umans often find it more comforting to perceive the actions of others and change around them as the result of simple choices and actions taken by others rather than part of a complex series of dependencies and interactions."

They're happy to be left alone

"You're certainly right about wanting to be left alone," said Badger.

"Exactly," said Owl. "You badgers want to be left to your own devices, sort your own issues and live with some certainty that things will continue without interruption by others, no matter how well meaning they may be. Umans are often the same, preferring to resolve their own issues, regarding individuals from outside of their group as a potential threat and someone who couldn't possibly understand their world or how it works."

They tend to be short-sighted

"OK, so I'm short-sighted," said Badger. "But is that what you meant?"

"Well, not really," said Owl. "What I meant was that you badgers don't tend to think long term. Umans call it recency bias, where every day decisions are simply based on short-term evidence and short-term reward; often ignoring longer term incentives, trends, or interests."

They're generally good natured if a bit hairy arsed!

They're a little bit greedy

They've seen change come and go

"What about the last three then?" said Badger.

"Well, you badgers are a fun group of animals to be around, good natured, a bit boisterous but generally warm-hearted. Umans aren't much different when they're with their own. Because of this short-term outlook, however, a quick reward is always going to be favoured over something in the future;

"'Snails tomorrow' as Jethro would put it," said Badger.

"Exactly"
"So finally, I put that you badgers had seen change come and go," said Owl. "Think about

what's happened here on the Levels. Way back in 1957 they started on the first station and no doubt your ancestors noticed some activity but kept their heads down until it died down and the station was built and in operation. Then again ten years later the same thing happened. This time a bit further away from the old den but no doubt loud noises all night and warnings about the need to move. In the end, things calmed down and life went back to normal again. Now in 2017 things have started up again and this time they seem closer?" "Too right," said Badger. "Those Umans are all over the place day and night."

"Exactly", said Owl. "I'm sure most of the older heads around the den said keep your heads down and this will pass again?"

"That's' exactly what they said around the tunnels and I'm sure the younger folk were hoping that they were right."

Owl stepped back and they looked at the whole list of badger traits:

- They live in family groups

- They are comfortable with routine; they're 'sett' in their ways!

- They can be fierce when cornered

- They see the world in black and white

- They're happy to be left alone

- They tend to be short-sighted

- They're generally good natured if a bit hairy arsed!

- They're a little bit greedy

- They've seen change come and go

Badger had been busily scribbling in his notebook.

"Can I just check my understanding with you, Owl, because this is interesting, have I got this right?" Reading from his book he asked, "You're saying then that families and teams are really important and give us a sense of identity?"

"Yes," said Owl. "And routines and habits dictate our behaviours?"

"Exactly. We can be fierce when we're threatened before we even understand what the change might be?"

"Not can be, will be," said Owl laughing.

"Are you are also saying that most of us like to see things simply and like things to be simple even if most of the time they aren't?"
"Yes, that's right. All of us prefer to see the world as a more predictable place than it actually is."

"I really can see that. Us badgers like to be left alone to sort our own issues and I don't know a single one of us who likes the interference of others from outside. I can see from the reactions of the others to the new station that they want to keep their heads down rather than grasp the nettle and move. This good natured and greedy point is spot on and that gets a few of us into trouble every now and again!"

Owl just smiled. "The final point of about change coming and going is exactly the conversation we have at the Shurton Arms over a pint of cider, night after night, despite the Umans getting closer and closer to the den."

"Right then," said Owl. "Clearly those Umans knew a bit about badgers when deciding how to move you lot. Tell me, Badger, why did you choose to follow the trail of chestnuts that night instead of heading off to Shurton as usual?" "Well, I guess I did it because I like nuts?"

"OK," said Owl. "What if, instead, there had been a huge sign that said 'Go to Cross Elms. It's Lush', would you have gone?"

"Not blooming likely," said Badger looking curious. "What are you getting at, Owl?"

"Well, when badgers decide what to do, they weigh up whether the consequences of whether what they're about to do will suit them. So, in your case, the prospect of a chestnut was worth a quick delay on your journey and then finding each time that there was another one just a bit further out of your way was enough to take you to Cross Elms that night."

Owl went across to the wall and wrote on the wall.

Positive or negative (P/N)

Immediate or future (I/F)

Certain or uncertain (C/U)

"What does that mean, Owl?" Badger asked.

"Well," said Owl, "making up your mind to do something isn't all that simple and we all quickly weigh up three things before we proceed with one course of action or another.
Firstly, are we going to get something we want or something we don't want, i.e. is the outcome going to be positive or negative for us? In your case, this was the prospect of chestnuts which you regarded as positive."

Then we decide whether we going to get it now or later. The promise of loads of worms later in the night at Shurton was not as powerful as the prospect of a chestnut now. I'm afraid we're all wired to go for instant, rather than delayed, gratification.

Finally, whether or not we're certain we're going to get what we want also plays heavily on our minds. Yes, there might be loads of worms in Shurton Woods but your excellent nose meant that you could smell out the next nut without too much difficulty. On balance, you were more certain that following your nose would give you the reward you were after.

Even if there had been ten signs asking you to go to Cross Elms you would've been unlikely to go because the reward, whilst presumably positive, is future and uncertain. Not strong enough, I'm afraid, to make you hike up the hill in the dead of night.

Those Umans knew that the prospect of a positive, immediate, and certain small reward would be enough to get you to follow the trail of nuts," said Owl. "What's more, keeping the trail fresh, night after night, only encouraged you to be more certain that following the path would be rewarding. By the way, thirteen nights of following a nut trail were probably enough to permanently change your night-time routine!"

Badger wrote in his book.

Choices are based on consequences NOW, rather than the prospect of future rewards.

"Interestingly enough, there's another way to get folk to do what you want but it needs continuous policing. Let me give you an example. Now, Jethro's got a fine collection of walking sticks in his rooms. Have you ever been tempted to sneak in and give them a look over?"

"Not blooming likely," said Badger.

"Why is that?" said Owl.

"Well he might be old but he's quiet and quick on his paws. He'd be bound to catch you and a wallop from one of his sticks would come sharp."

"Exactly," said Owl. "It's the prospect of a negative, immediate, and certain consequence of sneaking into his rooms that is sufficient to stop you doing it."

"What if you knew Jethro had headed out to the Shurton Arms for the night? Then might you be tempted to sneak in and have a look?" said Owl.

"Well, to be honest," said Badger, looking sheepishly at the floor, "that's exactly what I've done."

"What's the difference then?" said Owl.

"I suppose that as the chances of being caught go down then I'm more willing to give it a go?" "Yes, that's right. As soon as the prospect of punishment, or something negative, happening to you becomes in the future or increasingly uncertain then the more likely it is that you'll do what you want rather than what Jethro wants; which is for you to stay out of his room! When we talk later about the fences that the Umans put up to stop you getting back to the old den we'll see that the prospect of a night digging under the fence was enough to stop even Jethro bothering. Again, digging under the fence represented a negative, immediate, and certain consequence of arduous digging all night with no real prospect of getting home after all that effort. In other words, the chances of getting back to the old den had become positive, future, and uncertain and so not a great incentive for us to dig all night!"

Badger chewed his pencil again and wrote

Negative consequences can be as effective as positive ones. It's how quickly they happened and how certain an individual is that they will happen.

"Shall we talk about the link between this idea about consequences driving behaviours and our brains?" said Owl.

"Sounds interesting," said Badger, by now sitting up and looking at the wall.

"Let's look at what happens when you get something you want. How does it make you feel?"

"Great," said Badger.

"Do you know why?"

"No."

"Let me explain." Owl went back to the wall and wrote:

Brain Chemicals

Endorphins – Analgesic

Dopamine – Achievement

Selfish

Serotonin – Appreciation

Oxytocin – Amour

Social

Cortisol – Alarm

Adrenaline - Action

Survival

"Let me explain a bit about these chemicals," said Owl, "as they're the basic building blocks of our behaviour. The first are nature's painkillers, endorphins. They enable you to push your body beyond a place where it hurts. In evolutionary terms, these allowed you to outrun foxes and go further in search of food, water, or a mate than your body was actually fit to do.

If you've been out on a long strenuous hunt for food you will have experienced the effect of endorphins as the 'high' you feel after it's over. You'll know only too well that, as your endorphins recede to normal levels, this feeling will be replaced by sore muscles the day after.

Now the second one is dopamine; it creates a strong sense of achievement for our actions and it's the building block of our habits. Dopamine is self-driven and highly addictive. We can create our own hits of dopamine from the most minor of our achievements. For badgers, it's nature's method of getting you to return to plentiful sources of water and food. Every time you found one of those chestnuts, you gave yourself a quick lovely dose of dopamine.

So, you can see that just the anticipation of a series of small dopamine hits was enough to lead you to discover the den in Cross Elms Woods. In the life of those 'Umans, their addiction to dopamine is being satisfied by an ever-increasing list of personal achievements such as beating their satnavs, hitting KPIs, doing extra reps in the gym, treating themselves to something nice, getting the high score on their computer games, etc. etc.

These two chemicals drive essentially selfish behaviour in badgers and Umans alike but luckily, we've other chemicals that act to draw us together into cohesive groups.

The first one is serotonin and it's what binds

groups of badgers together. It's the tribal drug as it creates a sense of appreciation enabling you to form social groups and tribes. None of you badgers can survive alone; your successes as a species have been as a result of your ability to form social groups.

We're naturally drawn towards others who show their appreciation of us and our efforts. Even the smallest gesture of gratitude can trigger the warm glow of serotonin within us. As addictive as dopamine, serotonin is the fuel behind teamwork. Look what happened when you told Arthur about Cross Elms, how did it make you feel when he was delighted that you took him along?"

"It felt great," said Badger.

"Well, that's you giving yourself a gert big jollop of serotonin!

The second drug in this group I've drawn up on the wall is oxytocin. This drug creates a sense of connection to others. It supports social bonding and the development of strong personal relationships. I refer to it as the 'love drug' but it is much more than the driving force for you to mate. When mixed with serotonin, it is the very foundation of trust, without which we simply you would not be on the planet today.

"Let me ask you a question, Badger. How do you feel when you're in your bed at night in the den?"

"I feel safe and relaxed," said Badger extending his toes towards the fire and wondering whether he'd get into his bed at all by sunrise.

"Why is that?"

"Well, I suppose I know that others will be listening out for foxes and weasels, ready to spring into action, if needed."

"How do you feel if you don't make it back here and you have to sleep out in the wood?" Well, between you and me, Owl, it's terrifying!"

"I can well imagine," said Owl. "We'll talk about the drugs that try to keep you safe in a moment, but you can see that when you're in the den and you know that the others have your back not only can you sleep but it also means you're confident they'll keep the fires going, guard the stores and generally look after the place. You can only feel that way if oxytocin is released in your brain.

So we've talked about the personal chemicals that make us do things for ourselves – endorphins and dopamine – I've also mentioned the group chemicals that make it pleasant and essential to be with others – serotonin and oxytocin – and now I want to talk about the ones that are designed to keep us alive."

Suddenly there was a crash of plates outside the room. Badger leapt off his chair and put his nose out into the corridor. "Nothing to worry about," he said and slumped back in his chair.

"Now where were we, Owl?"

"Talking about the brain chemicals that are designed to keep us alive," said Owl. "Let me ask you when you got up to look into the corridor just now did you decide to do it or did it sort of happen automatically?"

"To be honest, Owl, I was heading towards the door wondering why I'd bothered. I knew it was just one of the others dropping a plate."

"That's really interesting and exactly an example of the next chemical I wanted to talk about, which was cortisol. When potential danger is detected, say a crash outside of the room, then your brain secretes a drug called cortisol that has loads of different effects but essentially prepares our bodies for danger. One of the first things it does is inhibits your neural network."

"What does that mean, Owl?" asked Badger quizzically.

"Well, because we have a number of pre-wired responses to danger, which over the course of evolution have served us well, our brain switches to solely focus on the immediate danger, it cuts off the thinking brain - the neocortex – in simple terms we work on autopilot; just as you did when you leapt up from your chair just now.

You can imagine that in everyday life, autopilot is not always a good thing; it brings up learned behaviour based on primitive fight, flight or freeze reactions; our pre-wired tactics; the only thought when these are triggered is how to stay safe. Have you ever had Jethro bustle in here and ask you if you can put your hands on a pick axe? What happens?"

"Well most of the time I can lay my hands right on one but when he's in here, I'm so focused on what he might say or do whilst he's here I often can't find the blooming thing."

"Exactly," said Owl "Most of us find that when we're worried about the potential actions of someone in authority, or the reaction of our peers that we find it hard to do day to day things that otherwise we would have little difficulty in completing. This is the effect of cortisol in shutting down the thinking part of your brain and focusing you on survival. I suspect that when you're asked for a pick axe your response is I'll bring it over to you later?"

"Yes, that's right," said Badger. "As soon as he's gone, I can find it. It's a strange thing, now you come to mention it."

"Yes, as the cortisol declines in your brain your neocortex comes back on line, you can think clearly and then find it."

"The other problem with this cortisol is that it creates a climate where no one cooperates and there's no trust. The key to survival is reaction speed and any delay created by our inquisitive brains could be the difference between life and death. For us, this is relevant every day and for the Umans, it was relevant on the plains and savannahs of their early existence.

For Umans in their 21st-Century organisations, the effects of cortisol on behaviour can be catastrophic. When they perccive potential danger to themselves, Umans fall back to learned behaviour. They repeat old mistakes and by operating on autopilot can make fundamental errors."

"This is a really interesting," said Badger. "Are you saying then that by just making us feel safe we can reduce the unhelpful effects of cortisol?"

"Exactly. It helps us step out of autopilot and think clearly. Amazingly, it's the only thing required to create true collaboration, teamwork and engagement in any organisation; it's a magic bullet!"

"Have you ever been in an actual fight, Badger?" asked Owl.

"Well, some time ago. Why do you ask?"
"What's your memory of it?" asked Owl.

"All I remember is what I call the 'Red Mist' descending and in I went. I wasn't going to let any of those weasels take our den so they were going to have it!"

"Well, that takes us on to the final drug in our list, which is adrenaline. This drug prepares our muscles for action. It creates a sense of strength that allows us to take action against threat. When it's released into the body it prepares us for action by constricting blood vessels, which then increases blood pressure, heart rate, and breathing rate. These changes in our system, along with the action of cortisol within our brains, trigger the fight/freeze/flight response."

Badger sat back and looked at his notes. He'd written:

Brains and Chemicals

Endorphins = go further
Dopamine = create habits
Serotonin = tribal and appreciation
Oxytocin = relationships
Cortisol = autopilot
Adrenaline = ready for action

Badger leapt up again and looked at the list. He pointed to 'Dopamine' and asked, "Are you saying then that each time I found a honey-covered nut it wasn't just the taste I enjoyed?"

"Exactly," said Owl. "Each time you ate one, you had a sense of achievement and that spurred you on to Cross Elms. What's more, when you got there, you found a massive source of dopamine; then when the family turned up serotonin and even good old oxytocin came into play.

Those 'Umans knew they had to create at least one of three things to get you lot to move home voluntarily," said Owl. "They either needed to make your lives easier, more stimulating, or more rewarding."

Owl wrote those three things on the wall.

Make the change

Easier
Stimulating
Rewarding

"I see," said Badger. "Finding the trail of nuts that led here every night meant I really couldn't be bothered to go over to Shurton Woods anymore and once we discovered the store of food here, well, I set up home pretty quickly."

"Exactly," said Owl. "I'm afraid all of us, and those Umans, are biased towards things that are easier and, therefore, we are more resistant to activities and behaviours that involve a degree of effort and challenge. After all, effort uses up valuable brain resources that could be deployed elsewhere or saved for emergencies."

"Right," said Badger looking thoughtful. "I must admit, finding the new den and exploring it with Arthur was really interesting and in some places like over there." He gestured at an alcove he'd created to house his antique sticks. "I built that myself to keep an eye on my collection and make the room feel more like my own. Got to say I enjoyed every minute and, when I stepped back to look at what I'd done, felt proud of my work; even Arthur said he'd never seen a better stick store."

"There you are", said Owl, "dopamine and serotonin in action. We're all drawn to activities that we perceive to be stimulating, interesting, novel, or fun. We rapidly lose interest and motivation with tasks and situations we perceive to be mundane, repetitive, and boring."

"So how has the move been rewarding then?" asked Badger.

"Well," said Owl, "this is a bit more complicated. Look around, what do you think of this room?"

"Well it's very comfortable, very, comfortable indeed," said Badger.

"Achieving a new place to live that suits you

well is an example of what we call an 'extrinsic reward.' In fact, each of those chestnuts was a small extrinsic reward in itself.

There's another sort of reward called 'intrinsic."

"What's that then?" said Badger.

"Well, think about how it felt when Arthur agreed with you that Cross Elms was a 'lush' place to live and stayed over with you those first few nights? Those feelings are what those Umans would call 'intrinsic', that is, freely given appreciation from others. The same feeling you had when the others had all decided to join you here and generally appreciated what you'd found."

Badger scratched his hairy chin. "So, you're saying those Umans knew that if they wanted us to move they would need to make it easier for us to stay here, make living here more interesting than the boring routine at homes, and make it more rewarding; or a combination of all three and then we'd move!"

"Exactly," said Owl.

"Well, swipe me," said Badger falling back into his armchair and absentmindedly chewing a dried slug from the bowl on his side table. In his notebook, he'd written,

"make things easier, more interesting, more rewarding".

"What's more," said Owl. "They knew that if they could make you feel safe in your new home by making it waterproof, secure from foxes, and with a constant food supply, your family would soon start pulling together, make the changes necessary to suit themselves, and settle down to a new life here in Cross Elms."

"OK," said Badger, fixing Owl with a short-sighted stare. "Why put the fence up then and why the one-way door?"

"Great question," said Owl and wrote, 'Remember: change is Scary' on the wall.

"Do you remember when you were in the Shurton Arms with your 'associates' a few months ago and Sid the landlord let you know that they'd run out of cider?"

"Do I ever," said Badger twitching his nose at the thought.

"Do you remember how you felt?" said Owl.

"Well, at first I thought I'd misheard him but when it was clear that he'd actually said they had no cider my second thought was this is a cruel joke he was playing on me."

Owl started writing on the wall. He drew a curve and wrote Shock then Denial at the start of the curve.

"What next?" she asked.

"Well, I said to him, 'Stop joking and blooming well pour me a pint'. I remember feeling a bit annoyed and was wondering why after twenty years behind the bar and with the same group of badgers coming in here night after night he couldn't get enough stock in. It's not like we're more than three miles from the orchard for goodness sake."

"What then?" asked Owl whilst writing Anger on the wall.

"Well, I remembered why I had gone in and didn't want to storm out and try and find another pub in Stringston or Kilton because I didn't know anyone there."

Owl wrote Depression on the wall at the bottom of the curve.

 "Do you know," she said, "that being with your 'associates' or your 'in group', is probably the single biggest reason why people don't change? That's why getting Arthur to come with you and persuading everyone else to make the move to Cross Elms was really important."

"So, are you saying the wall was put up to get everyone to the new den?" said Badger.
"Well, in part," said Owl. "Let's just finish the story about you and your pint of cider. What happened next?"

"Well, Sid said to me 'Why not try some Mendip ale?' He pointed out that it was only from a few miles away, that it was brewed by the same folk who brewed the cider, and was the same price."

"What did you do?" said Owl, already writing Explore on the wall.

"Well, I said I'd give it a go," said Badger, "and, blow me, it was quite nice. In fact, since that day, I only drink the Mendip ale. The cider plays havoc with my insides!" Owl wrote Accept and Integrate to complete the curve.

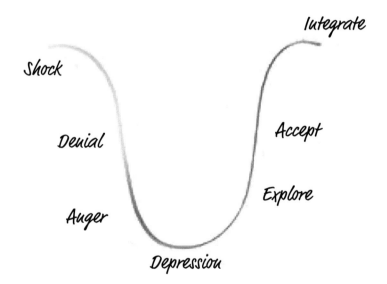

Shock

Integrate

Denial

Accept

Anger

Explore

Depression

"Believe it or not, every time we experience a change we all go through these feelings," said Owl. "Some go through them quicker than others and prior experience of change can make the process easier. So, for example, what would happen if Sid ran out of Mendip Ale one night?"

"Well," said Badger "I've been looking at his Quantock Stout, so I'd probably give that a go, to be honest."

"Exactly," said Owl. "Once we've experienced a change, and it's gone OK, we find it easier to accept another as long as it's not too different."

"Why's that then?" said Badger.

"Because we all make sense of our world by deciding how it is!"

Badger looked puzzled.

"Well, let's call this your Map of the World," she said, drawing a globe on the wall. "We all carry one round with us and in a tight family such as yours, they're all pretty similar. When something happens that conflicts with the way we thought our lives would be then we usually bury our heads even further underground, hope it will go away, or dismiss it. This is simply because changing your Map of the World is actually scary and, the further away the new change is from your map, the scarier it becomes."

"Aha," said Badger. "Is that why, despite the new rooms, the warmth, and the food here at Cross Elms, some of the older badgers hankered for the old den?"

"Exactly," said Owl. "The change for them –the prospect of moving– was scarier than for others. Their map of the world, formed over many years, had been challenged more than most and so a fence was necessary to keep them in Cross Elms whilst they came to terms with the change.

That fence is a Negative, Immediate, and Certain consequence of trying to get back home," she said pointing at the list of consequences on the wall. "Digging under the fence is hard work, it's hardly interesting, and, as for the reward, it was uncertain. Bear in mind that everyone else would have been here in Cross Elms with their feet up!"

Badger yawned. The sun was rising above Cross Elms Wood and he'd had a tough night of thinking. In his book he'd written

The same change can be more scary for some badgers than others; to stop those who are particularly worried going back make things difficult, boring and unrewarding.

"So," he said. "What do you think is at the core of the approach the 'Umans took?"

"Well," said Owl. "They know badgers, don't they? They know about brain chemicals and, finally, they know about riding donkeys!"

"Got the first two but what do you mean about the donkey?" said Badger, sitting up once again and sucking on an earthworm like a piece of spaghetti. Owl drew a picture of a donkey on Badger's wall: on the top of it was a badger attempting to ride it.

"OK," she said. "If you're attempting to make a donkey go left and she'd rather carry on straight who is ultimately going to win?"

Badger thought and eventually said, "Well, I guess the donkey. It's much stronger than the rider?"

"Exactly," said Owl. "The secret is in three simple steps that brings everything together," and wrote the following on the wall.

How to Move a Donkey

Give it simple instructions

Make going in any other direction more difficult

Toss it the odd carrot now and again!

"I see," said Badger. "So those 'Umans laid a trail of honey-covered sweet chestnuts, which was simple to follow, and they did that every night so that I was pretty sure they'd be there, and that this would be much easier than heading over to Shurton Woods?"

"Yes," said Owl. "These were your simple instructions, easy directions, and your version of the odd carrot now and again!" said Owl, now laughing along with Badger who was quietly chuckling to himself.

"Well, blow me," he said.

Outside the sun appeared over the hills of
Exmoor lighting up the Welsh mountains on
the other side of the Bristol Channel. Badger
looked back at his book and said to Owl. "Well
that's quite enough for one night, thank you,
Owl. I'm not sure if I've got it all but wow!
What an interesting set of ideas."

Owl beamed at his friend and thought, yes, that
had been a great night.

LEADER'S CHECKLIST FOR CHANGE...

Why should we change? How will the future result or the endpoint be better than our current reality?

What will be easier, more stimulating, and/or more rewarding for each individual when the change has happened?

What will be the first/smallest/easiest steps to take?

How will I provide positive reinforcement for doing 'the right things'?

How will I sustain the positive reinforcement beyond the first few successes or first few days?

How will I make it more difficult, less stimulating, and/or less rewarding for those who slip back into old habits?

How much choice/autonomy can I give to those going through the change?

MODELS AND THEORY

Brain Chemistry

Our brains run on electrical impulses and chemicals. Behavioural research and neuroscience are increasingly demonstrating strong links between certain neurotransmitters and the impact they have upon our actions and behaviours.

In his book, Leaders Eat Last (2014), Simon Sinek gives a fantastic description of how our dependence upon these neurotransmitters evolved. Chief amongst these are what we refer to as 'The Big Six'.

"Our ancestors of the Palaeolithic era lived in times where resources were either scarce or hard to come by. Imagine if every time we felt hungry, we had to go hunting for a few hours...with no guarantee that we'd catch anything. Odds are our species would not have survived very well with a system like that. And so our bodies, in an effort to get us to repeat behaviours that are in our best interest, came up with a way to encourage us to go hunting and gathering on a regular basis instead of waiting until we are starving." Simon Sinek (Leaders Eat Last)

Our Selfish Drivers

The first two chemicals, endorphins and dopamine, work to get us to achieve what we need to as individuals. They drive and enable us to go farther, work harder, and persevere in our quest to find food, build shelters, and get things done. As such, Sinek labels them 'selfish'.

Endorphins are nature's painkillers. They enable us to push our bodies beyond physical comfort. In evolutionary terms, endorphins allowed us to outrun our predators and go further in search of food, water, or a mate.

Anyone who exercises properly will have experienced the effect of endorphins as the high they feel after strenuous exercise only to be replaced by sore muscles and various aches and pains the day after exercise as our endorphins recede to 'normal' levels.

Dopamine is the building block of habits. It creates a sense of achievement for our actions.

Dopamine is self-driven and highly addictive. We can create our own hits of dopamine from the most minor of achievements. Where once it was nature's method of getting us to return to plentiful sources of water and food, in our abundant lives today, we see our addiction to dopamine being satisfied by an ever-increasing list of personal achievements such as beating the satnav, hitting our KPIs, doing those extra reps in the gym, treating ourselves to something nice, getting the high score on computer games, etc., etc.

Our Social Drivers

Being selfish is all well and good and, to a great degree, necessary for our survival as a species, but we wouldn't have lasted long without the support, protection, and collaboration of others. To accomplish this, our bodies created serotonin and oxytocin to create social bonds, trust, and relationships that helped us nurture our young.

Serotonin creates bonds and relationships, enabling us to form social groups and tribes. Homo sapiens cannot survive alone. Our success as a species has been as a result of our ability to form social groups. Key to this group-formation process is serotonin. We are naturally drawn towards others who show their appreciation of us and our efforts. Even the smallest gesture of gratitude can trigger the warm glow of serotonin within us. As addictive as dopamine, serotonin differs in that it can only be driven through interaction with others, thus driving us into a 'social dependency'.

Oxytocin creates the feelings of trust, friendship, affection, and love. It is released when we experience close contact and skin-to-skin contact with others…yes, there's more to shaking hands, high-fives, knuckle-bumps and hugs than we think! But it's not just a 'pink and fluffy, feel-good' drug; without oxytocin, we would have no empathy with others, no feelings for others, and, therefore, no relationships, collaboration, or trust…the very building blocks of our social bonds.

Our Survival Drivers

Our world used to be, and in our more ancient brain physiology, still is, a dangerous place. To help us survive the 'circle of life', our bodies gave us two more chemicals, which trigger our survival responses.

Cortisol is our neural inhibitor. It puts us in a state of high alert. Part of the human condition is our constant state of inquisitiveness. We are continually thinking about things, questioning, exploring, and creating. These are all useful skills in times of safety but become potentially lethal to us when we are presented with danger. At times of great danger, we need to be able to switch off our inquisitive minds and get on with surviving. Cortisol is our chemical off-switch that effectively closes down our neocortex, enabling us to redirect our mental resources into survival tactics.

Adrenaline – OK, so it's not a neurochemical but it sure helps us survive! Our first response to threat is the release of cortisol to the brain; in partnership, our adrenal glands release adrenaline into our system to prepare our muscles for action. Adrenaline gives us a sense of strength and stamina to defend ourselves or get out of the way quickly.

Selfish	Dopamine	Creates a sense of achievement for our actions. The building block of habits.
Selfish	Endorphins	Nature's painkillers. They enable us to push ourselves beyond physical comfort.
Social	Serotonin	Creates a sense of appreciation between people, enabling us to form social groups and tribes.
Social	Oxytocin	Creates a sense of connection to others. Supports social bonding and the development of strong personal relationships.
Survival	Cortisol	Creates a sense of high alert. Closes down the functions of the neocortex to engage the fight or flight reflex.
Survival	Adrenaline	Prepares our muscles for action. Creates a sense of strength that allows us to take action against threats.

ABC and PIC/NIC analysis

In his book, Bringing Out the Best in People (1994), Aubrey Daniels introduces the ABC of behaviour:

Antecedent (The trigger or stimulus for behaviour)
Behaviour
Consequence (What happens to us as a result of our chosen behaviour)

Daniels proposes that all behaviour is a result of the consequences to us rather than the triggers and stimuli.

Businesses have historically failed to effectively and sustainably influence behaviour through repeated efforts to enforce and reinforce antecedents, leading to more and more rules, policies, procedures, signs, and auditors. Through the intelligent use of consequences, Daniels presents us with a methodology to more effectively and, most importantly, *sustainably* influence our behavioural choices day-by-day and minute-by-minute.

R+ Positive reinforcement - Getting something I want
R- Negative reinforcement - Not getting/avoiding something I don't want
P+ Punishment - Getting something I don't want
P- Extinction - Not getting something I want

Positive Reinforcement (R+) – *I get something I want*

When we receive praise, recognition, thanks, appreciation, awards, treats, dopamine, or serotonin for our actions, we experience the impact of positive reinforcement. Not only does this feel nice, it also begins to lay foundations for creating habits. We are so addicted to the chemical rush these small ceremonies give us that we are almost hard-wired to repeat them.

Consider how we encourage our children to learn to walk and talk or learn new skills...every step is met with applause, appreciation and encouragement. Now contrast this with how we treat learning and the development of new skills in the workplace. Just because we get older does not mean we no longer crave and blossom under the same conditions.

Negative Reinforcement (R-) – *I don't get something I don't want*

I don't want to be embarrassed, made to do difficult tasks, feel singled out, rejected, hurt or punished, so when my actions avoid these uncomfortable situations, I experience negative reinforcement. The net effect of this is that I learn to deliver just enough to avoid any uncomfortable outcome.

This type of behaviour we see most often in highly critical businesses where the focus is continually on errors, 'failures' and 'where we need to improve'. Whilst it is a working approach, the decline in attention and effort leaves very little room for error.

Punishment (P+) – *I get something I don't want*

On the surface, this looks relatively simple to explain. My actions or inactions lead to a punitive experience like disciplinary action, taking the minutes at meetings for being late, etc. After a while, the experience of punishment has a diminishing impact and so, performance declines.

There is a darker side to this where leaders inadvertently 'punish' our best people.

When your star performer finishes his/her tasks ahead of schedule, do we give them the rest of the day off or load them up with another task? When a reluctant child tells you they've finished their homework (at last!), how do we respond, with praise and appreciation or a lecture on how it was in your day?

How often do we see well-intentioned leaders 'punishing' their star performers?

Extinction (P-) – *I don't get something I want*

We choose and enact our behaviours in the expectation of some reaction. When we don't experience the reaction we imagined, then our willingness to try again exponentially declines.

We see the benefits of this where teachers and parents 'ignore' or pay no attention to badly behaved children in the classroom. By giving attention to other 'better behaved' children, the teacher effectively 'extincts' the disruptive behaviour.

And the dark side of extinction... pretty much everyone in your organisation wants to do a decent job. Some will be 'stars' and perform exceptionally, some will fall short of the mark for various reasons, but the vast majority of our people fall somewhere in-between. Unfortunately, busy leaders will ignore this overwhelming majority of good people in favour of managing the stars and problem children, and, in so doing, disengage good people through extinction.

The diagram below shows that when we get more of the things we want (positive reinforcement) we deliver a greater amount of discretionary effort as opposed to when we avoid something we don't want – negative reinforcement – where we do only as much as is necessary... leaving very little margin for error.

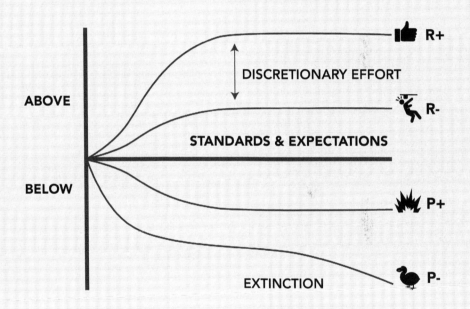

Heading beneath the standards line, we see that punishment leads to a decline in delivery standards and, worst of all, extinction (not getting the recognition we want) quickly leads to a complete cessation of effort.

Behavioural Analysis

Our behaviour can have a number of consequences for us:
Positive or **negative** (P/N)
Immediate or **future** (I/F)
Certain or **uncertain** (C/U)

NB: It is important to understand that consequences should be viewed as neither 'good' nor 'bad'; they are simply consequences.

In terms of *positive* and *negative* consequences, they are for the **individual only**. The decision is based solely upon the impact to the decision maker and no other party.

Immediate and *future* are measured in the timespan from **the point of decision**, so, basically, anything that does not impact at the moment of choice is by definition, a future consequence.

Certain or *uncertain* is a measure of the degree of confidence the individual has that a consequence will **absolutely happen**, based upon their experience.

Consequences that are proven to have the biggest impact upon behaviour are those that are Immediate and Certain…PICs and NICs.

For any behaviour to happen and be sustained there must, therefore, be a number of PICs driving the person towards the behaviour and a few NICs keeping the person away from behaving differently.

When influencing behaviour, we have the option to reverse this 'status quo' by making the old behaviour less *positive*, less *immediate*, or less *certain* (or a combination of all three). Alternatively, we can create strategies to similarly reduce the impact and influence of the NICs

Put more simply, humans will choose more strongly to do things that are *easier*, more *stimulating/enjoyable* or more *rewarding* and chose to avoid things that are perceived to be *difficult*, *boring*, or less *rewarding*.

The source code of behaviour

Our behaviour, whilst complex in construction and unique to every one of us, shares some commonalities with others. These commonalities are the result of biases. These operate below our conscious thought processes and have evolved over millennia to provide the neural shortcuts that allow us to operate effectively when we need to focus on more 'important and pressing matters'. Three biases, which are most commonly found at the heart of human behavioural choices and worth exploring, are easy vs. difficult, stimulating vs. boring and reward vs. threat.

Easy or Difficult? – As a species, we are biased towards things which are easier and, therefore, more resistant to activities and behaviours that involve a degree of effort and challenge. This is the reason why going for that run on a rainy day requires a serious application of willpower! And why diets, fitness, and quitting 'bad' habits are always the top of our New Year Resolutions…whilst they are aspirational and desirable, the degree of effort, application and challenge we encounter when undertaking the behavioural change can quickly eclipse the benefits we perceived when making the resolution.

Stimulating or boring? – Like the curious monkeys we are at origin, we are also drawn to activities that we perceive to be interesting, novel, or fun. And will actively avoid anything we perceive to be unnecessarily mundane or predictable.

Take a look at the work of The Fun Factory on YouTube whose members challenge themselves to create novelty and stimulation in the most mundane of tasks – from picking up litter to taking the stairs over the elevator – in order to encourage people to change their behaviour.

Rewarding or threatening? – We experience a sense of gaining a 'reward' at two levels: extrinsic – gifts and tokens of appreciation that are given to us such as bonuses, awards, etc., and intrinsic – the sensations created within ourselves as a result of neurochemistry when we create a sense of achievement (dopamine) or appreciation (serotonin), the rush of adrenaline when we rise to a challenge, and oxytocin when we make friends and fall in love. Activities and behaviours that remove the potential for reward become less favoured and those with increasingly less potential for reward can even be perceived as threatening and are therefore avoided at all costs.

So, to put it as simply as possible… if you want more of a specific behaviour from your people, make it easier for them to do it, more stimulating, more rewarding or a combination of all three, and they are more certain to do it! Alternatively, if you want your people to stop doing something, make it more difficult for them to continue to do it, less interesting, and a lot less rewarding!

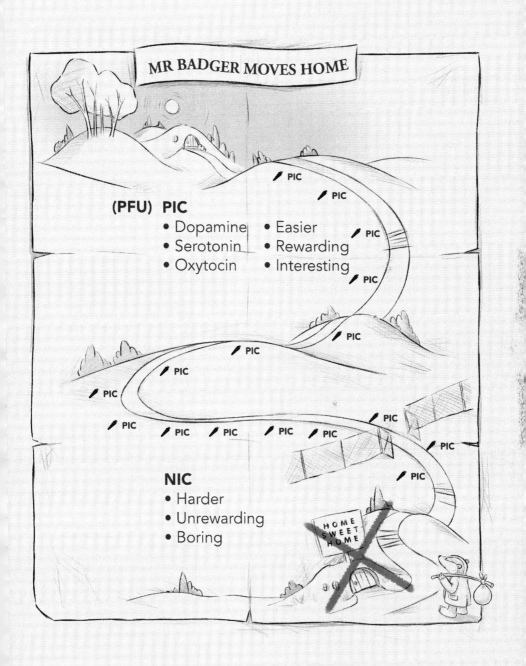

If you'd like to hear more please visit our website **www.ctlconsult.com** or look us up on LinkedIn.

Printed in Great Britain
by Amazon